A Prayer for Our Country

Words to Unite and Inspire Hope

Senate Chaplain Barry Black

Illustrated by **Kim Holt**

ZONDERKIDZ

A Prayer for Our Country
Copyright © 2022 by Barry Black
Illustrations © 2022 by Kim Holt

Requests for information
should be addressed to:

Zonderkidz, 3900 Sparks Dr. SE,
Grand Rapids, Michigan 49546

Hardcover ISBN 978-0-310-77123-4

Ebook ISBN 978-0-310-77126-5

Design: Diane Mielke

Printed in South Korea

22 23 24 25 26 27 /SAM/ 13 12 11 10 9 8 7 6 5 4 3 2 1

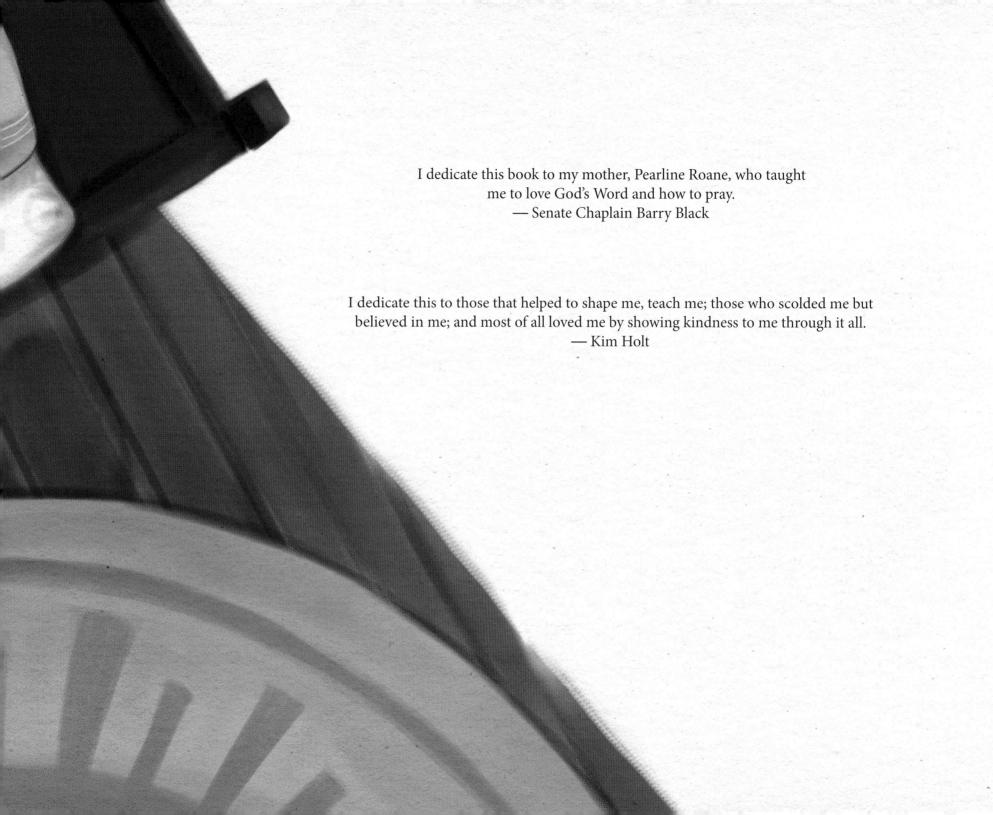

I dedicate this book to my mother, Pearline Roane, who taught
me to love God's Word and how to pray.
— Senate Chaplain Barry Black

I dedicate this to those that helped to shape me, teach me; those who scolded me but
believed in me; and most of all loved me by showing kindness to me through it all.
— Kim Holt

Eternal God, who commands the sun to appear,

we come to You today with thankful hearts.

Lord, we are grateful for the breath of the morning, for the strength that lies in us,

for friends, and for family.

We praise You for the glory of Your creation.

For the songs of the birds, the beauty of the flowers, and every evidence of your love.

Loving Father, we who are blessed with clothes to wear, food to eat, and homes to shelter us

ask You to bless the people who are hungry, hurting, and hopeless.

Use us as Your hands, feet, eyes, ears, and heart to bring joy to others.

Lord, lead us as a shepherd directs the sheep. Teach us to use words wisely.

Remind us that harsh words hurt, while kind words heal.

May our words refresh others so that we will be refreshed ourselves.

Strong God, give us the ability to see Your divine image in every human being.

Remind us that You do not love some people better than others,

and may this knowledge unite us as a human family.

Great God, we admit that we face big problems.

Sometimes we feel scared, hurt, and even lost.

It's easy for us to feel overwhelmed by the work we need to do.

But we know that You are always with us.

Give us wisdom to understand that You are stronger
than any challenge we face.

Lord, thank You for choosing to call
us Your children.

Show us how to live so that this country may be a better place, and help us to do our best whether there is anyone to see it or not.

Thank You for always being with us,

causing the shadows of night to flee.

We pray in Your loving name.

Amen.